EQUIPMENT

MAINTENANCE

LOG

SERVICE RECORD

DATE	MALFUNCTIONING EUIPMENT	NATURE OF DEFECT	SERVICE PROVIDER	DATE OF LAST SERVICE	SERVICE DATE	PRONOSIS

SERVICE RECORD

DATE	MALFUNCTIONING EUIPMENT	NATURE OF DEFECT	SERVICE PROVIDER	DATE OF LAST SERVICE	SERVICE DATE	PRONOSIS

SERVICE RECORD

DATE	MALFUNCTIONING EUIPMENT	NATURE OF DEFECT	SERVICE PROVIDER	DATE OF LAST SERVICE	SERVICE DATE	PRONOSIS

SERVICE RECORD

DATE	MALFUNCTIONING EUIPMENT	NATURE OF DEFECT	SERVICE PROVIDER	DATE OF LAST SERVICE	SERVICE DATE	PRONOSIS

SERVICE RECORD

DATE	MALFUNCTIONING EUIPMENT	NATURE OF DEFECT	SERVICE PROVIDER	DATE OF LAST SERVICE	SERVICE DATE	PRONOSIS

SERVICE RECORD

DATE	MALFUNCTIONING EUIPMENT	NATURE OF DEFECT	SERVICE PROVIDER	DATE OF LAST SERVICE	SERVICE DATE	PRONOSIS

SERVICE RECORD

DATE	MALFUNCTIONING EUIPMENT	NATURE OF DEFECT	SERVICE PROVIDER	DATE OF LAST SERVICE	SERVICE DATE	PRONOSIS

SERVICE RECORD

DATE	MALFUNCTIONING EUIPMENT	NATURE OF DEFECT	SERVICE PROVIDER	DATE OF LAST SERVICE	SERVICE DATE	PRONOSIS

SERVICE RECORD

DATE	MALFUNCTIONING EUIPMENT	NATURE OF DEFECT	SERVICE PROVIDER	DATE OF LAST SERVICE	SERVICE DATE	PRONOSIS

SERVICE RECORD

DATE	MALFUNCTIONING EUIPMENT	NATURE OF DEFECT	SERVICE PROVIDER	DATE OF LAST SERVICE	SERVICE DATE	PRONOSIS

SERVICE RECORD

DATE	MALFUNCTIONING EUIPMENT	NATURE OF DEFECT	SERVICE PROVIDER	DATE OF LAST SERVICE	SERVICE DATE	PRONOSIS

SERVICE RECORD

DATE	MALFUNCTIONING EUIPMENT	NATURE OF DEFECT	SERVICE PROVIDER	DATE OF LAST SERVICE	SERVICE DATE	PRONOSIS

SERVICE RECORD

DATE	MALFUNCTIONING EUIPMENT	NATURE OF DEFECT	SERVICE PROVIDER	DATE OF LAST SERVICE	SERVICE DATE	PRONOSIS

SERVICE RECORD

DATE	MALFUNCTIONING EUIPMENT	NATURE OF DEFECT	SERVICE PROVIDER	DATE OF LAST SERVICE	SERVICE DATE	PRONOSIS

SERVICE RECORD

DATE	MALFUNCTIONING EUIPMENT	NATURE OF DEFECT	SERVICE PROVIDER	DATE OF LAST SERVICE	SERVICE DATE	PRONOSIS

SERVICE RECORD

DATE	MALFUNCTIONING EUIPMENT	NATURE OF DEFECT	SERVICE PROVIDER	DATE OF LAST SERVICE	SERVICE DATE	PRONOSIS

SERVICE RECORD

DATE	MALFUNCTIONING EUIPMENT	NATURE OF DEFECT	SERVICE PROVIDER	DATE OF LAST SERVICE	SERVICE DATE	PRONOSIS

SERVICE RECORD

DATE	MALFUNCTIONING EUIPMENT	NATURE OF DEFECT	SERVICE PROVIDER	DATE OF LAST SERVICE	SERVICE DATE	PRONOSIS

SERVICE RECORD

DATE	MALFUNCTIONING EUIPMENT	NATURE OF DEFECT	SERVICE PROVIDER	DATE OF LAST SERVICE	SERVICE DATE	PRONOSIS

SERVICE RECORD

DATE	MALFUNCTIONING EUIPMENT	NATURE OF DEFECT	SERVICE PROVIDER	DATE OF LAST SERVICE	SERVICE DATE	PRONOSIS

SERVICE RECORD

DATE	MALFUNCTIONING EUIPMENT	NATURE OF DEFECT	SERVICE PROVIDER	DATE OF LAST SERVICE	SERVICE DATE	PRONOSIS

SERVICE RECORD

DATE	MALFUNCTIONING EUIPMENT	NATURE OF DEFECT	SERVICE PROVIDER	DATE OF LAST SERVICE	SERVICE DATE	PRONOSIS

SERVICE RECORD

DATE	MALFUNCTIONING EUIPMENT	NATURE OF DEFECT	SERVICE PROVIDER	DATE OF LAST SERVICE	SERVICE DATE	PRONOSIS

SERVICE RECORD

DATE	MALFUNCTIONING EUIPMENT	NATURE OF DEFECT	SERVICE PROVIDER	DATE OF LAST SERVICE	SERVICE DATE	PRONOSIS

SERVICE RECORD

DATE	MALFUNCTIONING EUIPMENT	NATURE OF DEFECT	SERVICE PROVIDER	DATE OF LAST SERVICE	SERVICE DATE	PRONOSIS

SERVICE RECORD

DATE	MALFUNCTIONING EUIPMENT	NATURE OF DEFECT	SERVICE PROVIDER	DATE OF LAST SERVICE	SERVICE DATE	PRONOSIS

SERVICE RECORD

DATE	MALFUNCTIONING EUIPMENT	NATURE OF DEFECT	SERVICE PROVIDER	DATE OF LAST SERVICE	SERVICE DATE	PRONOSIS

SERVICE RECORD

DATE	MALFUNCTIONING EUIPMENT	NATURE OF DEFECT	SERVICE PROVIDER	DATE OF LAST SERVICE	SERVICE DATE	PRONOSIS

SERVICE RECORD

DATE	MALFUNCTIONING EUIPMENT	NATURE OF DEFECT	SERVICE PROVIDER	DATE OF LAST SERVICE	SERVICE DATE	PRONOSIS

SERVICE RECORD

DATE	MALFUNCTIONING EUIPMENT	NATURE OF DEFECT	SERVICE PROVIDER	DATE OF LAST SERVICE	SERVICE DATE	PRONOSIS

SERVICE RECORD

DATE	MALFUNCTIONING EUIPMENT	NATURE OF DEFECT	SERVICE PROVIDER	DATE OF LAST SERVICE	SERVICE DATE	PRONOSIS

SERVICE RECORD

DATE	MALFUNCTIONING EUIPMENT	NATURE OF DEFECT	SERVICE PROVIDER	DATE OF LAST SERVICE	SERVICE DATE	PRONOSIS

SERVICE RECORD

DATE	MALFUNCTIONING EUIPMENT	NATURE OF DEFECT	SERVICE PROVIDER	DATE OF LAST SERVICE	SERVICE DATE	PRONOSIS

SERVICE RECORD

DATE	MALFUNCTIONING EUIPMENT	NATURE OF DEFECT	SERVICE PROVIDER	DATE OF LAST SERVICE	SERVICE DATE	PRONOSIS

SERVICE RECORD

DATE	MALFUNCTIONING EUIPMENT	NATURE OF DEFECT	SERVICE PROVIDER	DATE OF LAST SERVICE	SERVICE DATE	PRONOSIS

SERVICE RECORD

DATE	MALFUNCTIONING EUIPMENT	NATURE OF DEFECT	SERVICE PROVIDER	DATE OF LAST SERVICE	SERVICE DATE	PRONOSIS

SERVICE RECORD

DATE	MALFUNCTIONING EUIPMENT	NATURE OF DEFECT	SERVICE PROVIDER	DATE OF LAST SERVICE	SERVICE DATE	PRONOSIS

SERVICE RECORD

DATE	MALFUNCTIONING EUIPMENT	NATURE OF DEFECT	SERVICE PROVIDER	DATE OF LAST SERVICE	SERVICE DATE	PRONOSIS

SERVICE RECORD

DATE	MALFUNCTIONING EUIPMENT	NATURE OF DEFECT	SERVICE PROVIDER	DATE OF LAST SERVICE	SERVICE DATE	PRONOSIS

SERVICE RECORD

DATE	MALFUNCTIONING EUIPMENT	NATURE OF DEFECT	SERVICE PROVIDER	DATE OF LAST SERVICE	SERVICE DATE	PRONOSIS

SERVICE RECORD

DATE	MALFUNCTIONING EUIPMENT	NATURE OF DEFECT	SERVICE PROVIDER	DATE OF LAST SERVICE	SERVICE DATE	PRONOSIS

SERVICE RECORD

DATE	MALFUNCTIONING EUIPMENT	NATURE OF DEFECT	SERVICE PROVIDER	DATE OF LAST SERVICE	SERVICE DATE	PRONOSIS

SERVICE RECORD

DATE	MALFUNCTIONING EUIPMENT	NATURE OF DEFECT	SERVICE PROVIDER	DATE OF LAST SERVICE	SERVICE DATE	PRONOSIS

SERVICE RECORD

DATE	MALFUNCTIONING EUIPMENT	NATURE OF DEFECT	SERVICE PROVIDER	DATE OF LAST SERVICE	SERVICE DATE	PRONOSIS

SERVICE RECORD

DATE	MALFUNCTIONING EUIPMENT	NATURE OF DEFECT	SERVICE PROVIDER	DATE OF LAST SERVICE	SERVICE DATE	PRONOSIS

SERVICE RECORD

DATE	MALFUNCTIONING EUIPMENT	NATURE OF DEFECT	SERVICE PROVIDER	DATE OF LAST SERVICE	SERVICE DATE	PRONOSIS

SERVICE RECORD

DATE	MALFUNCTIONING EUIPMENT	NATURE OF DEFECT	SERVICE PROVIDER	DATE OF LAST SERVICE	SERVICE DATE	PRONOSIS

SERVICE RECORD

DATE	MALFUNCTIONING EUIPMENT	NATURE OF DEFECT	SERVICE PROVIDER	DATE OF LAST SERVICE	SERVICE DATE	PRONOSIS

SERVICE RECORD

DATE	MALFUNCTIONING EUIPMENT	NATURE OF DEFECT	SERVICE PROVIDER	DATE OF LAST SERVICE	SERVICE DATE	PRONOSIS

SERVICE RECORD

DATE	MALFUNCTIONING EUIPMENT	NATURE OF DEFECT	SERVICE PROVIDER	DATE OF LAST SERVICE	SERVICE DATE	PRONOSIS

SERVICE RECORD

DATE	MALFUNCTIONING EUIPMENT	NATURE OF DEFECT	SERVICE PROVIDER	DATE OF LAST SERVICE	SERVICE DATE	PRONOSIS

SERVICE RECORD

DATE	MALFUNCTIONING EUIPMENT	NATURE OF DEFECT	SERVICE PROVIDER	DATE OF LAST SERVICE	SERVICE DATE	PRONOSIS

SERVICE RECORD

DATE	MALFUNCTIONING EUIPMENT	NATURE OF DEFECT	SERVICE PROVIDER	DATE OF LAST SERVICE	SERVICE DATE	PRONOSIS

SERVICE RECORD

DATE	MALFUNCTIONING EUIPMENT	NATURE OF DEFECT	SERVICE PROVIDER	DATE OF LAST SERVICE	SERVICE DATE	PRONOSIS

SERVICE RECORD

DATE	MALFUNCTIONING EUIPMENT	NATURE OF DEFECT	SERVICE PROVIDER	DATE OF LAST SERVICE	SERVICE DATE	PRONOSIS

SERVICE RECORD

DATE	MALFUNCTIONING EUIPMENT	NATURE OF DEFECT	SERVICE PROVIDER	DATE OF LAST SERVICE	SERVICE DATE	PRONOSIS

SERVICE RECORD

DATE	MALFUNCTIONING EUIPMENT	NATURE OF DEFECT	SERVICE PROVIDER	DATE OF LAST SERVICE	SERVICE DATE	PRONOSIS

SERVICE RECORD

DATE	MALFUNCTIONING EUIPMENT	NATURE OF DEFECT	SERVICE PROVIDER	DATE OF LAST SERVICE	SERVICE DATE	PRONOSIS

SERVICE RECORD

DATE	MALFUNCTIONING EUIPMENT	NATURE OF DEFECT	SERVICE PROVIDER	DATE OF LAST SERVICE	SERVICE DATE	PRONOSIS

SERVICE RECORD

DATE	MALFUNCTIONING EUIPMENT	NATURE OF DEFECT	SERVICE PROVIDER	DATE OF LAST SERVICE	SERVICE DATE	PRONOSIS

SERVICE RECORD

DATE	MALFUNCTIONING EUIPMENT	NATURE OF DEFECT	SERVICE PROVIDER	DATE OF LAST SERVICE	SERVICE DATE	PRONOSIS

SERVICE RECORD

DATE	MALFUNCTIONING EUIPMENT	NATURE OF DEFECT	SERVICE PROVIDER	DATE OF LAST SERVICE	SERVICE DATE	PRONOSIS

SERVICE RECORD

DATE	MALFUNCTIONING EUIPMENT	NATURE OF DEFECT	SERVICE PROVIDER	DATE OF LAST SERVICE	SERVICE DATE	PRONOSIS

SERVICE RECORD

DATE	MALFUNCTIONING EUIPMENT	NATURE OF DEFECT	SERVICE PROVIDER	DATE OF LAST SERVICE	SERVICE DATE	PRONOSIS

SERVICE RECORD

DATE	MALFUNCTIONING EUIPMENT	NATURE OF DEFECT	SERVICE PROVIDER	DATE OF LAST SERVICE	SERVICE DATE	PRONOSIS

SERVICE RECORD

DATE	MALFUNCTIONING EUIPMENT	NATURE OF DEFECT	SERVICE PROVIDER	DATE OF LAST SERVICE	SERVICE DATE	PRONOSIS

SERVICE RECORD

DATE	MALFUNCTIONING EUIPMENT	NATURE OF DEFECT	SERVICE PROVIDER	DATE OF LAST SERVICE	SERVICE DATE	PRONOSIS

SERVICE RECORD

DATE	MALFUNCTIONING EUIPMENT	NATURE OF DEFECT	SERVICE PROVIDER	DATE OF LAST SERVICE	SERVICE DATE	PRONOSIS

SERVICE RECORD

DATE	MALFUNCTIONING EUIPMENT	NATURE OF DEFECT	SERVICE PROVIDER	DATE OF LAST SERVICE	SERVICE DATE	PRONOSIS

SERVICE RECORD

DATE	MALFUNCTIONING EUIPMENT	NATURE OF DEFECT	SERVICE PROVIDER	DATE OF LAST SERVICE	SERVICE DATE	PRONOSIS

SERVICE RECORD

DATE	MALFUNCTIONING EUIPMENT	NATURE OF DEFECT	SERVICE PROVIDER	DATE OF LAST SERVICE	SERVICE DATE	PRONOSIS

SERVICE RECORD

DATE	MALFUNCTIONING EUIPMENT	NATURE OF DEFECT	SERVICE PROVIDER	DATE OF LAST SERVICE	SERVICE DATE	PRONOSIS

SERVICE RECORD

DATE	MALFUNCTIONING EUIPMENT	NATURE OF DEFECT	SERVICE PROVIDER	DATE OF LAST SERVICE	SERVICE DATE	PRONOSIS

SERVICE RECORD

DATE	MALFUNCTIONING EUIPMENT	NATURE OF DEFECT	SERVICE PROVIDER	DATE OF LAST SERVICE	SERVICE DATE	PRONOSIS

SERVICE RECORD

DATE	MALFUNCTIONING EUIPMENT	NATURE OF DEFECT	SERVICE PROVIDER	DATE OF LAST SERVICE	SERVICE DATE	PRONOSIS

SERVICE RECORD

DATE	MALFUNCTIONING EUIPMENT	NATURE OF DEFECT	SERVICE PROVIDER	DATE OF LAST SERVICE	SERVICE DATE	PRONOSIS

SERVICE RECORD

DATE	MALFUNCTIONING EUIPMENT	NATURE OF DEFECT	SERVICE PROVIDER	DATE OF LAST SERVICE	SERVICE DATE	PRONOSIS

SERVICE RECORD

DATE	MALFUNCTIONING EUIPMENT	NATURE OF DEFECT	SERVICE PROVIDER	DATE OF LAST SERVICE	SERVICE DATE	PRONOSIS

SERVICE RECORD

DATE	MALFUNCTIONING EUIPMENT	NATURE OF DEFECT	SERVICE PROVIDER	DATE OF LAST SERVICE	SERVICE DATE	PRONOSIS

SERVICE RECORD

DATE	MALFUNCTIONING EUIPMENT	NATURE OF DEFECT	SERVICE PROVIDER	DATE OF LAST SERVICE	SERVICE DATE	PRONOSIS

SERVICE RECORD

DATE	MALFUNCTIONING EUIPMENT	NATURE OF DEFECT	SERVICE PROVIDER	DATE OF LAST SERVICE	SERVICE DATE	PRONOSIS

SERVICE RECORD

DATE	MALFUNCTIONING EUIPMENT	NATURE OF DEFECT	SERVICE PROVIDER	DATE OF LAST SERVICE	SERVICE DATE	PRONOSIS

SERVICE RECORD

DATE	MALFUNCTIONING EUIPMENT	NATURE OF DEFECT	SERVICE PROVIDER	DATE OF LAST SERVICE	SERVICE DATE	PRONOSIS

SERVICE RECORD

DATE	MALFUNCTIONING EUIPMENT	NATURE OF DEFECT	SERVICE PROVIDER	DATE OF LAST SERVICE	SERVICE DATE	PRONOSIS

SERVICE RECORD

DATE	MALFUNCTIONING EUIPMENT	NATURE OF DEFECT	SERVICE PROVIDER	DATE OF LAST SERVICE	SERVICE DATE	PRONOSIS

SERVICE RECORD

DATE	MALFUNCTIONING EUIPMENT	NATURE OF DEFECT	SERVICE PROVIDER	DATE OF LAST SERVICE	SERVICE DATE	PRONOSIS

SERVICE RECORD

DATE	MALFUNCTIONING EUIPMENT	NATURE OF DEFECT	SERVICE PROVIDER	DATE OF LAST SERVICE	SERVICE DATE	PRONOSIS

SERVICE RECORD

DATE	MALFUNCTIONING EUIPMENT	NATURE OF DEFECT	SERVICE PROVIDER	DATE OF LAST SERVICE	SERVICE DATE	PRONOSIS

SERVICE RECORD

DATE	MALFUNCTIONING EUIPMENT	NATURE OF DEFECT	SERVICE PROVIDER	DATE OF LAST SERVICE	SERVICE DATE	PRONOSIS

SERVICE RECORD

DATE	MALFUNCTIONING EUIPMENT	NATURE OF DEFECT	SERVICE PROVIDER	DATE OF LAST SERVICE	SERVICE DATE	PRONOSIS

SERVICE RECORD

DATE	MALFUNCTIONING EUIPMENT	NATURE OF DEFECT	SERVICE PROVIDER	DATE OF LAST SERVICE	SERVICE DATE	PRONOSIS

SERVICE RECORD

DATE	MALFUNCTIONING EUIPMENT	NATURE OF DEFECT	SERVICE PROVIDER	DATE OF LAST SERVICE	SERVICE DATE	PRONOSIS

SERVICE RECORD

DATE	MALFUNCTIONING EUIPMENT	NATURE OF DEFECT	SERVICE PROVIDER	DATE OF LAST SERVICE	SERVICE DATE	PRONOSIS

SERVICE RECORD

DATE	MALFUNCTIONING EUIPMENT	NATURE OF DEFECT	SERVICE PROVIDER	DATE OF LAST SERVICE	SERVICE DATE	PRONOSIS

SERVICE RECORD

DATE	MALFUNCTIONING EUIPMENT	NATURE OF DEFECT	SERVICE PROVIDER	DATE OF LAST SERVICE	SERVICE DATE	PRONOSIS

SERVICE RECORD

DATE	MALFUNCTIONING EUIPMENT	NATURE OF DEFECT	SERVICE PROVIDER	DATE OF LAST SERVICE	SERVICE DATE	PRONOSIS

SERVICE RECORD

DATE	MALFUNCTIONING EUIPMENT	NATURE OF DEFECT	SERVICE PROVIDER	DATE OF LAST SERVICE	SERVICE DATE	PRONOSIS

SERVICE RECORD

DATE	MALFUNCTIONING EUIPMENT	NATURE OF DEFECT	SERVICE PROVIDER	DATE OF LAST SERVICE	SERVICE DATE	PRONOSIS

SERVICE RECORD

DATE	MALFUNCTIONING EUIPMENT	NATURE OF DEFECT	SERVICE PROVIDER	DATE OF LAST SERVICE	SERVICE DATE	PRONOSIS

SERVICE RECORD

DATE	MALFUNCTIONING EUIPMENT	NATURE OF DEFECT	SERVICE PROVIDER	DATE OF LAST SERVICE	SERVICE DATE	PRONOSIS

www.ingramcontent.com/pod-product-compliance
Lightning Source LLC
Chambersburg PA
CBHW080309180526
45167CB00006B/2728